Perversion of
LOVE

Understanding the Enemy's Attack
on Your Love Language

CRYSTAL WRIGHT ADAMS

ISBN 978-1-0980-8130-0 (paperback)
ISBN 978-1-0980-8131-7 (digital)

Christian Faith Publishing, Inc.
832 Park Avenue
Meadville, PA 16335
www.christianfaithpublishing.com

Printed in the United States of America

Contents

Acknowledgments

To my one and only Momala,

Thank you for breaking the cycles you did for our family. Thank you for choosing grace, though you rarely saw it modeled. Thank you for the gift of your hugs and kisses, though you weren't taught to give them. Thank you for your consistency, your support, and your love because without those things, some cycles would have continued. You forged a new path for our family, and because of your courage, you have positioned us to completely change the course of future generations. Know that the seed you planted in obedience will produce a harvest of fruitfulness for generations to come. Thank you, and we love you!

Love,
All of us!

The 5 Love Languages:
Setting the Stage

Dr. Gary Chapman and Dr. Ross Campbell wrote a book called *The 5 Love Languages of Children* (2012) in which they discuss how important it is for children to *feel* loved. It is not enough for a child to hear "I love you"; they must *feel* love in order to receive it. The doctors found five primary ways that children *feel* loved: *words of affirmation, quality time, gifts, acts of service,* and *physical touch* (p. 26). They encouraged parents to identify the primary way or ways their child receives love and to be intentional about giving them love in these ways; they referred to this as "speaking" in the child's "love language" (p. 9). When first reading this book, I could not believe that what I considered to be the complex concept of love could be simplified into five basic "languages." Though the more I thought about it, the more accurate this idea became.

Based on the doctors' analysis, I determined that my love language as a child was absolutely *words of affirmation*; I lived and breathed by the encouragement and recognition of others, especially those seen as authority figures in my life. I decided to take Dr. Chapman's Love Languages Quiz as an adult to see if the results would be the same. (This is a good place for you to pause and take the quiz yourself if you haven't already.) My quiz revealed that both *quality time* and *acts of service* were my primary love languages. I registered the same score for both. This assessment was spot-on! It's not that I can't be alone or do things for myself, but when someone is willing to spend their time and energy on me, I truly *feel* loved. Encouragement and recognition from a loved one no longer hold as much weight for me as their actions do. Still, the quiz confirmed that my second highest scoring love language was indeed *words of affirmation*. *Words of affirmation* never went away but perhaps evolved within the context of my life experiences.

Dr. Chapman also wrote another book about love entitled *The 5 Love Languages: The Secret to Love that Lasts* (2010). This book was geared toward couples attempting to strengthen and even save their marriages by identifying their spouse's love language and giving them love in that way. Want to take a crack at what those five love languages are? You guessed it! The very same love languages we speak in as children: *words of affirmation, quality time, gifts, acts of service,* and *physical touch.* I find it interesting that Dr. Chapman wrote his book for adults first and then realized the importance of how these same love languages apply to children. Though we may not be consciously aware of the love languages we are speaking and that are being spoken to us as children, it is evident that they follow us into adulthood. Our love languages may evolve, but they are still rooted in those primary ways that we needed to *feel* loved as children. I believe God created us like this intentionally.

Before Jesus left earth, He gave us what we call the Great Commission (Matthew 28:19–20), which is to *go and spread the Gospel to all nations.* I believe that the way God designed us to love is directly related to our assignments in carrying out this commission. Our love language is a powerful tool that God uses in and through us to win souls for His kingdom. It is the way we relate and connect with the people we're assigned to. It isn't a coincidence that Jesus's final and greatest commandments were to *love*: love God with all your heart and love your neighbor as yourself. In fact, He said that all other commandments the Father had given were based on these two (Matthew 26:36–40). This is where the concept of love gets sticky for a lot of us—even Christians. *"Love your neighbor as yourself?"* Hmm? Why is that so hard for us?

Many of us struggle in some way to give the love and grace that God has given us to other people. I know I'm guilty of this, and I have a theory as to why this struggle exists. We've learned that the foundation of our love language is built in childhood and stays with us through adulthood. We also know that God's greatest commandments are to love Him and love our neighbors. He created us to love in a certain way because that love—our love language—is what will help us be most effective in spreading the Gospel. The greatest commandments are how we fulfill the Great Commission, which is ultimately our purpose on this earth. Since God works through His people, this assignment is crucial for establishing His kingdom on earth; and anything God establishes, Satan attempts to destroy. So why do we struggle with loving our neighbors as ourselves? Because we don't truly know how to love ourselves, and I believe it all started in childhood…

Chapter 1

Perversion: The Setup

The number one goal of the enemy is to destroy God's plan for our lives: "Be sober-minded; be watchful. Your adversary the devil prowls around like a roaring lion, seeking someone to devour" (1 Peter 5:8). I believe his favorite weapon of destruction is perversion. Google defines perversion as "the alteration from its original course, meaning or state to a distortion or corruption of what was first intended." The "original course" in our lives is God's ultimate purpose for it. Satan seeks to corrupt that purpose or to stop it from being achieved altogether. I'll use a personal example to illustrate this point.

God gave me the gifts of writing and speaking. From a very young age, I demonstrated an advanced ability to articulate my words whether written or spoken. I now know that it was always God's plan for my life for me to speak to people about His Word and to write words that would help His people overcome their spiritual struggles. When I was a child, the enemy came to destroy that purpose. As a young girl, music spoke to my soul. I loved music more than anything. To be quite honest, I used music to fill a deficit of love in my life (we'll discuss that a little later), and so music became that love. One day, I decided to write my own song. I turned on one of my favorite artists' tracks and wrote my own lyrics to it, rearranging the melody over the original beat. It was amazing. It *felt* amazing. I was in my zone, and the words and melody flowed from me so effortlessly; of course they did—I was created to write. But instead of using my gifts to glorify God, the enemy played on my need for affirmation and recognition, and I chose to pursue life as a famous singer/songwriter. I wanted everyone to know the words I wrote and to love them as much as I did because that would mean they loved me too. I started an R&B singing group with my best friend and two other girls. We spent the next six years working with a producer, performing in local events, and recording original tracks. Almost all the lyrics were written by me, and I also arranged most of the melodies. I thought I was living my dream, but eventually our group broke up and the reality that I might never be famous—that people would never know my lyrics—started to set in. By this time, I was in my freshman year of college and had just began dating my now ex-husband. I was still grieving the death of my dream when he came along to reinforce every negative thought I had about my gifts, talents, and capabilities. If I had been a better writer, we would have made it. If I had arranged a better melody, we would have been noticed. I was convinced that not being famous—not being recognized—was proof that I didn't truly possess these gifts—*my* gifts. I didn't write again until I turned thirty, and it took another five years for me to believe that I could write this book.

Sometimes the enemy attacks us in such a way that we become the very antithesis of what we were created to be. Let's look at Paul for this example. Most of us know the story of Paul in Acts chapter 9. At this time in his life, he was called Saul, and Saul was the number one "hater" in the New Testament. He persecuted Christians like it was an Olympic event and he was Michael Phelps (no disrespect intended, just drawing the comparison). One day on the road to Damascus, Saul had an encounter with Jesus that left him blind for the next three days. When Saul arrived in Damascus, the Lord called upon His disciple Ananias to heal him. Ananias was apprehensive because of the many evil things Saul had done to God's people, but the Lord told him, "Go without fear: for he is a special vessel for me, to give to Gentiles and Kings and to the Children of Israel the knowledge of My Name" (Acts 9:15 BBE). The Word of God tells us that God created us for a purpose which He prepared for us in advance (Ephesians 2:10). This means that before Saul ever set his mind to condemn and kill Christians, God had always planned for him to be a vessel in spreading the Gospel. If this is true, how did Saul go so far off from the path that was set before him? Perversion. Though not much is known about Paul's own childhood, his trade as a tent maker (a common laborer) would suggest that he came from humble beginnings as opposed to a wealthy or aristocratic background. What *is* apparent from Paul's earlier years is that he was very smart and quite ambitious, and I suspect, like me, his love language may have been words of affirmation. This presented the perfect opportunity for the enemy to infiltrate Paul's life in the form of education by the Pharisees. Pharisees believed nonbiblical traditions were as important as the written Bible, and they persecuted those who did not uphold them. Before his conversion, Paul considered himself an expert in these traditions (Galatians 1:13–14) and even referred to himself as the best Jew and Pharisee (Philippians 3:4–6). The enemy used Paul's need to be affirmed—to *feel* worthy—to lead him down the exact opposite path for which he was created.

Though Satan is not omniscient, he was once a high-ranking angel of God and he, more than anyone, knows why we were created. Armed with this knowledge, he studies us to determine how God will use us for this purpose. When he zeroes in on our assignment, he is determined to destroy it; just ask Adam and Eve. The enemy is subtle and crafty. He will approach you in a manner that won't seem out of place: perhaps as a snake in the garden or a devoutly religious education in pharisaical law or even as your parents in your childhood. Satan wants to enter your heart, your mind, your speech, and even your body. And just as God works through people, so does the enemy—and the devil doesn't care who he uses. The easiest way for him to infiltrate your life and start to derail your purpose is through your relationship with your parents.

We've learned that we receive love in five primary ways. Take this time to think about the primary love language you speak:

1. Is it words of affirmation (someone telling you how special or valued you are)?
2. Is it quality time (someone giving you their undivided attention)?

3. Is it gifts (tokens of appreciation)?
4. Is it acts of service (someone sacrificing their time and energy for you)?
5. Or perhaps physical touch (a warm embrace from a loved one)?

Now, think about how your parents showed their love to you when you were a child. I'm willing to bet that a large percentage of us had at least one parent who didn't give us love in our love language which, as we now know, means we likely weren't receiving their love. It's true that most people give love the way that they learned it, or in the way they want to receive it, and our parents are no exception. This gives the enemy an opening to slither into our childhoods and distort the ways we are given and receive love. It can also create a cycle of generations failing to receive the love they need, making it almost impossible for them to learn to love themselves. It's no wonder we struggle with the idea of truly loving someone else. The danger in this is that we can become trapped in these cycles which potentially detour us from our ultimate purpose. But, as the saying goes, the first step in solving a problem is to recognize and acknowledge that it exists.

I believe acknowledgment is also the first step in breaking a generational cycle. After that, we must identify the root cause of our cycle or problem so that we can determine the strategies needed to overcome it. That's just what this book aims to do. I want to help us recognize the generational cycles we may be trapped in and understand that the likely root cause is the perversion of our love language starting in our childhoods. Since all of us receive love differently, the enemy will attack us in different ways, but there are some common tactics he uses depending on our love language. If we can recognize these tactics for what they were or are, we can start the process of breaking the cycles in our lives, the lives of our children, and, hopefully, the generations to follow.

Chapter 2

Words of Affirmation: Because You're Amazing... Just the Way You Are

Words are extremely powerful in communicating love. The Bible says that "words kill and words give life; they're either poison or fruit—you choose" (Proverbs 18:2 *The Message Bible*). Our words can be either poison or fruit; poison weakens and destroys and fruit is often sweet, healthy, and helps to sustain life. When words are affectionate; endearing; or full of praise, encouragement, and positive guidance, the person receiving them is being told that they are valued and cared for. According to *The 5 Love Languages of Children*, these words "nurture [a] child's inner sense of worth and security" (p. 47). Though the words themselves may be forgotten quickly, the love that was received (*felt*) when they were spoken can have long-lasting effects. When words are harsh, critical, and birthed out of situational frustration, they can cause a child to not only question their worth but their abilities too. As children, we tend to take everything said to us at face value. So imagine your parents, the ones that birthed you and were responsible for your well-being, consistently using words that tear down your spirit. If even your own parents expressed the worst about you, how could you ever begin to establish a sense of self-worth or arrive at a place of truly loving yourself? That's exactly what the devil wants—it's perversion.

If you were like me as a kid, you needed kind words, positive reinforcements, and gentle reassurances to not only know your worth but to *feel* that you were loved. This was evident to my mother when I was very young. After every achievement, no matter how big or small, I looked for the praise of my mother, and she always obliged. I never questioned whether my mother loved me. Regardless of my accomplishments, she always made me feel worthy of her praise—her love. This assurance motivated me to make her proud in every-thing I did. I thank God that my mother was well-versed in my love language. It was when I was only six years old that my dad entered the picture and the enemy began his attack. Can you guess what love language he was *not* fluent in?

I was a little girl who thrived on recognition and praise, and what I received from my dad was criticism and an almost constant reminder of my shortcomings; nothing was ever done well enough. In my adolescent mind, I concluded that my dad simply did not love me—not truly. Sure he helped to keep a roof over our heads and clothes on our backs, but he only did that because he had to—that's what dads did. It was the words he often spoke toward me that con-firmed he merely tolerated me. It was easy for me to subscribe to this belief because he was usually much kinder and gentler to my younger sister. I was "meatball legs" and she was "spaghetti legs." I was "Crys" and she was "babe." I was a "momma's girl" whom he appeared to resent, and she was "daddy's little girl." I quickly developed a com-plex that she was his favorite and that I was unworthy. The more I tried to win his affection, the more steadfast he appeared to deny me, and the more I resented my sister. As a result, my sister and I were not as close growing up as we are today. It's true we had very different personalities, but when I look back on where the major division in our childhood relationship presented itself, I can pinpoint it to when my dad joined our family. Before he came, I was my sister's protector. After he came, she became my greatest enemy.

The words that my dad chose to speak to me throughout my childhood and adolescence had ramifications beyond those seasons in my life. I developed a warped sense of self with the constant and overbearing self-view that there was always something wrong with me, something not up to par. This led to two very distinct behavioral responses. First, I started to become jealous of and dislike my sister, whom I saw as competition. In hindsight, I know I was simply masking my insecurities and misplacing my hurt and anger. Second, I believed that if I tried my hardest, I could get my dad to recognize my worth and he would finally give me the love and affirmation I so desperately desired. These coping mechanisms are things that I carried into adulthood. I now realize that every romantic relationship I've had in my adult life can be characterized by me trying to pull the love I desire out of a man who is either unwilling or incapable of giving it to me and then misplacing the hurt/frustration/anger it caused me onto some other woman. With my dad, it was my little sister. With my ex-husband, it was the women he dated before me or maybe a female coworker that I felt he treated better than me. With any man I've dated since then, regardless of how short- or long-lived the relationship, the same pattern repeated. And it was this unmet need for affirmation from my father that made me believe the dysfunction of my relationship with my ex-husband was normal. I never liked when my ex-husband spoke down to me, but that's what my father did. I hated it when my ex-husband would highlight my flaws, but that's what my father did. It broke my heart when my ex-husband would compare me to other women, but that's what my father did. This perversion of my love language made me justify the red flags that would ultimately become the finish line of my marriage—a cycle perpetuated by words.

The Bible tells us that we are responsible for choosing our words. So what happens when you have no choice in the words spoken to you? It starts with understanding that everything you're hearing that is the opposite of *God's Word* is an attack from the enemy. God clearly tells us His intentions for us in Jeremiah 29:11 *not to harm us, but to give us hope and a future*. If what we're experiencing is harming us physically, mentally, emotionally, or spiritually, it is not of God and is undoubtedly a tool of the enemy. This can include our own willful disobedience—yes, let that sink in…

Having analyzed my childhood as an adult, I know my dad gave me love the best way he knew how. He had experienced his own childhood hurts and, as the saying goes, "hurt people hurt people," which is what the devil is betting on. But knowledge is power, and if the Holy Spirit indwells in you, you already possess this power: "The Spirit of the Lord will rest on him—the Spirit of wisdom and of understanding, the Spirit of counsel and of might, the Spirit of the knowledge and fear of the Lord" (Isaiah 11:2 NIV). You may not have been able to choose the words that were spoken to you in your past, but you *can* choose to make different decisions moving forward. Choose to believe what God's Word says about you, what your Father in heaven believes about you rather than the harsh criticisms you may have received from your earthly parents. Remember that they are human, too, and dealing with hurt and brokenness like the rest of us. Choose to forgive them and give them the same grace God gave you by sending His Son to die on the cross. Then choose to break the cycle established in your childhood and, perhaps, even before that. Be intentional about speaking words of life over everyone you encounter, especially your children, so that they will always *feel* valued and never question your love for them. Help them to develop a strong sense of self-worth rooted in Christ, which cannot be shaken nor torn down by any man—least of all the enemy. In doing these things, in making these choices and being intentional about breaking cycles God's way, you will receive your healing and give God the glory, which is what we exist to do. Revelations 12:11 says that *we overcome the evil one with the blood of The Lamb and the* word *of our testimony*—our words. Words can kill or give life. Let your words give life to others in Christ. That's how we overcome!

Chapter 3

---- ∽ ----

Quality Time: All By Myself...
Don't Wanna Be

Quality time is perhaps the hardest of all the love languages to give. Why? Because *quality time* requires the most sacrifice on the part of the giver. You've probably heard your pastor or your favorite YouTube preacher tell you to seek God's presence: to sit undistracted in the presence of God so that you can be more aligned with Him in spirit and more in line with His will for your life. The Bible says to "seek ye first the Kingdom of God and His righteousness, and all of these things will be added unto you" (Matthew 6:33). This scripture is both a command and a promise. God promised us that if we seek Him first in everything we do, He will provide for all our needs. Why? Because obeying His commands is how we show God that we love Him (John 14:15 ESV), and He reciprocates that love toward us. Seeking God's presence essentially equates to spending *quality time* with Him. When we spend *quality time* with God, we're showing Him that we love Him through our obedience and the sacrifice of our time. The same can be said of those who love in *quality time*; when you love them in their love language, they *feel* loved because of the time you spent with them, and they will reciprocate that love toward you. But if we're honest with ourselves, I think we can all admit that we find spending quality time with God to be a difficult task despite the fact the He's always there (omnipresent). If that's true, how much harder is it for us to spend quality time with another human being who's not?

In our society, "time is money." We've built a culture around focusing our time and energy on things that will get us ahead. Whether it is getting ahead financially, positionally, or even materialistically, we busy our lives with the tasks and activities designed to get us there. This makes time an especially important commodity, and time is never more precious than in the life of a person who loves in quality time. For them, it is not that they can't be alone but that undivided attention from the giver makes them *feel* valued, important, and loved. If the person giving their time is preoccupied or distracted, the love will not be *felt*. These are the reasons why the enemy can so easily pervert the love language of quality time. He starts his attack in the childhood or adolescent stages aiming to corrupt the way the receiver both gives and receives love into adulthood.

When my ex-husband was a little boy, he spent a lot of time with his parents, especially his mother. I remember his childhood next-door neighbor telling me how he'd follow his mom around like a little duckling while she cooked, did her household chores, or worked in their garden. He himself would tell me about the solo trips he and his dad took to go fishing or visit family in Chicago. As an adolescent, he spent a lot of time with his friends whether it was staying over for dinner, spending the night, or even being invited to join their family outings. These were memories my ex-husband relished. You see, my ex-husband's primary love language is quality time. It makes perfect sense! All the happy memories he shared with me about his childhood were centered on the time spent with family and friends. From our first date, we never spent a single day away from each other if it was within our power to do so. Even if we were just lying around watching TV, he wanted me there with him. I didn't mind that at all because, as you now know, one of my primary love languages is also quality time. Honestly, his childhood sounded so great to me. I wish I could have been that close to my dad growing up. It wasn't until years later that I learned there was much more to the story. One of the reasons my ex-husband spent so much time with his friends was that his own family wasn't really close. Of course they all lived under the same roof, but "family dinners" consisted of everyone fixing a plate and then heading to their respective rooms to eat, not like the meals shared around the dinner table with his friends' families. Those fishing trips with his dad involved my ex-husband fishing in one spot while his dad fished in a different spot several feet away with limited interaction between the two of them. Most surprisingly was the abrupt ending to the time spent with his mom when he was only fifteen years old. My ex-husband was the only child still living at home and woke up one morning to discover his mom had left. He had no knowledge of where she had gone nor any way to contact her directly. He knew she had been unhappy in her marriage for years and understood her reasons for wanting to leave, but I don't think he will ever understand the reasoning behind the *way* she left him. If he wanted to contact his mother, the message was relayed through a family friend who refused to give my ex-husband his mom's new contact information. Though his mom faithfully sent him money each month, he had no idea where the money was being sent from or that his mom was in a completely different state at the time. His older siblings had moved out of their house and were focused on families of their own. His relationship with his dad remained as emotionally distant as it had always been—physically together but never truly interacting. His circle of friends was still there, but the interactions my ex-husband had with his family—his parents—during that time could not be characterized as "quality." Quite frankly, neither could the interactions leading up to that point. My ex-husband inherently desired closeness with his loved ones, to *feel* connected to them through their presence and shared experiences, but their actions, even if subconsciously, conveyed that he was not worth their time and effort. He had been abandoned figuratively and literally. It was the perfect scenario for the enemy to come in and try to completely distort the way my ex-husband processed love.

Whether he realized it or not, my ex-husband's interactions with his parents taught him that a person's own interests and desires came before anyone else—even family. While that didn't quell his inherent desire for quality time, it did cause him to develop the perspective that everyone—even family—was "disposable" or replaceable. Talk about perversion. If he treated everyone he was in a relationship with as though them being there didn't truly matter to him, how could he ever be close enough to them to truly *feel* loved? In my ex-husband's case, he became adept at keeping people physically close but never being vulnerable enough to where their departure would hurt him. In fact, since those he loved and wanted to be close to had historically left him, he went on the offensive and made sure to always have a "plan B" waiting in the wings; after all, it was only a matter of time before "plan A" came to an end. Any time there was conflict in our relationship, my ex-husband started lining up his plan B. Every single year of the twelve years we spent together was marked by my ex-husband wanting to break up, separate, or divorce (in response to an argument) so that he could pursue his "next best thing" (which he often did), only to want us to be together again. I called him out on this pattern, and his response was "Every new girl has been better than the last, so the next one will be better than you." He really believed this and voiced this belief consistently during our arguments over the topic. Because of the perversion of my own love language, I stuck by his side far longer than I should have, trying to prove I was worthy of the love I desired—his love. It wasn't until years after our marriage ended that I realized how the enemy had done his best to damage both of us before we ever knew the other existed. As I've already mentioned, "hurt people hurt people," and the enemy wants us all hurting by perverting the way we receive love so that we can continue the cycle of hurt in our own lives and the lives of others. After our marriage ended, my ex-husband continued jumping from one relationship to the next with little or no time in between. He continued to pursue the "next best thing," and it wasn't until he was nearly forty years old that he came to the realization that he had never truly learned how to love. I believe this was rooted in the lack of love through quality time from his parents. My ex-husband was a little boy who desired to spend quality time with his parents. He became a young man that consistently had quality time stripped away from him by the ones that were supposed to be there for him no matter what. This hurt, caused by the perversion of his love language, created a man that believed loving himself meant

22

throwing people away once he had found their newer, better replacement. Why? Because the abandonment he experienced told him that everyone was replaceable—even him.

If your love language is quality time, you may not have been abandoned by your loved ones, but maybe they were excessively busy and made everything a priority over you. Maybe they were present but always distracted or preoccupied with something other than you. Whether you realized it or not, all these actions could have subconsciously told you that you were not worthy of receiving love in the way you most desired—in the way you needed to *feel* it. This can have effects like preventing you from being close to others or keeping you in a toxic situation for the sake of having someone there. Either way, you have to take the time to discover the root cause which will require spending quality time with our Father in heaven. Sit in His presence—undistracted—and pray. Ask God to reveal to you the root of the perversion so that you can acknowledge it for what it is and begin the process of healing. Ask Him to heal those wounds suffered so long ago. Healing from that hurt can stop it from being passed on to others by you. It may be the first step on the journey to reclaiming your love language and, perhaps, getting you back on track for the life God always purposed for you. That purpose has always been to guide others, including your future generations, to Christ through love.

Chapter 4

Gifts: You Can't Buy Me Love

The Bible says that "every good and perfect gift is from above, coming down from the Father" (James 1:17). According to *The 5 Love Languages*, the giving and receiving of gifts can be a very powerful expression of love and even become a symbol of the love one person feels from another (p. 77). However, the love language of gifts is unique in that it is the only one that does not stand on its own. For the receiver to *feel* the love from a gift, it must be given in combination with one of the other four love languages (*quality time, acts of service, physical touch*, or *words of affirmation*). Because of His great love for us, our Father in heaven gave us the greatest gift of all: His Son, Jesus (John 3:16). Through the gift of His Son, God also gave us His *quality time* (Jesus's coming to earth as a man and His earthly ministry), *acts of service* (Jesus washing the disciples' feet and even His death on the cross), *physical touch* (Jesus's many healing miracles), and *words of affirmation* (Jesus's message of redeeming love). If God would have given us His Son without the combination of any of these other love languages, many may not have received His gift of salvation. This important qualifying factor is exactly how the enemy perverts the love language of gifts.

It can be tempting for someone who doesn't love in gifts to consider those that do superficial, shallow, and materialistic—the act of giving these people gifts can become obligatory. If you're that someone, then you are missing the connection that gifts have with the other love languages, and the devil is banking on this. No one *feels* loved if they believe someone gave them a gift out of obligation. Even God asks us not to give grudgingly or out of necessity for He loves a cheerful giver (2 Corinthians 9:7). If God Himself will not receive gifts (love) without the proper heart posture, how much more would we, full of human emotion, fail to receive that love? For a person who loves in gifts, it's not necessarily the object given that holds meaning, but what it represents. The gift tells the receiver that you love them enough to sacrifice your time, energy, or resources for them; that they are valued because of this sacrifice, and this object is the proof. So, what does the perversion of this love language look like? I believe the enemy has two primary tactics, and I've seen them play out firsthand with people in my own life.

The first time I met my stepdaughter, she was only four years old. She was an only child and teeming with imagination—the kind of imagination that kids who often play by themselves seem to develop. I remember how attached she became to me during that first meeting. She wanted me to do everything with her: play with Bratz dolls, paint her nails, watch the Disney Channel and let her style my hair. I have two little brothers that are only a year older than her, so I was practiced at interacting with and relating to young kids. Her mother and father (my ex-husband) divorced when she was very young. I recall a conversation between her and I when she was about eight years old where she revealed that she never knew her parents had been married. Apparently, I was the first person to confirm that for her. Her life, as far as she could remember, had always consisted of splitting her time between her mom and dad. In fact, due to her mother's military career and her parents' lack of cordiality with one another, my stepdaughter's life had largely been spent shuffling back and forth between her parents and various other family members on her mother's side. As my interactions with my stepdaughter continued, I started to notice a trend: every time she came to visit, she would ask for a new toy or some sort of treat. In turn, her father always obliged; whatever she asked for, she received. She began to expect the same from me, and she was not shy about asking me to buy her anything her little heart desired. I didn't know it at the time, but it's obvious to me now that my stepdaughter's primary love language was gifts. I didn't always respond to her in that love language. I much preferred to watch the cartoons and pretend to play "beauty shop," which made sense because quality time is one of my love languages. Her father, however, was well-versed in the language of gifts—or so it seemed at the time. It got to the point where my stepdaughter didn't even have to ask for gifts anymore. Her father proactively offered them and even went so far as to tell her that she wasn't expected to say "thank you" because as her father, he was supposed to get her what she wanted (obligation). I never agreed with this practice but reconciled that it was due to some sort of guilt he felt over not getting to see her as often as he wanted. Maybe that was a factor, but there was something else I started to pick up on. I noticed that whenever my stepdaughter would visit, my ex-husband would rely on me to be the one to spend time with her. He called it our "girl time," but "girl time" was more than just playing with dolls and painting nails. It included things like grocery shopping, taking her to my hair appointments, visiting with my parents (without my ex-husband present), and even taking her to school with me because her father had to work and "she could just color" while I was trying to pay attention to the professor's lecture. Still, whenever we returned from our "girl time," there was always a treat waiting for her or a quick trip to go buy her the item of her choice. I realized that my ex-husband seemed to be replacing the time he'd spend with my stepdaughter with gifts, and this practice continued as she grew older. Instead of spending quality time with her, he'd buy her games for her computer; and she'd stay in her room for hours, playing them by herself. Instead of greeting her with a hug when she got home from school, he bought her a dog that became her best friend and who never failed to greet her happily as soon as she walked through the door. Instead of being the primary person to teach her to drive, he paid for driving school and bought her a convertible Mustang. Instead of affirming that she was beautiful just as she was, he bought her whatever makeup and clothes she asked for to make her feel beautiful. The gifts my stepdaughter yearned for and received were not gift-wrapped properly; gifts must be wrapped in another love language for their meaning to be *felt*. As we now know, my ex-husband was suffering from the perversion of his own love language, but that doesn't change the effects his gift giving had on my stepdaughter. Children who genuinely love through gifts but only receive presents are not receiving love. Their sense of love is being distorted as they are conditioned to expect gifts in place of the love they truly desire. This was true for my stepdaughter. She expected gifts but didn't appear to appreciate them. She wanted gifts but grew to resent the person giving them. She didn't *feel* the love, so the gifts ultimately had no meaning to her. Children like this can grow into adults that display a lack of appreciation for the gifts they receive because of the obligatory nature with which they've always received them. While they innately desire these gifts, they have never *felt* true love in receiving them and, therefore, may never have truly *felt* loved—perversion. Does this sound like anyone you know? Contrary to what most people might think, you really can't buy love—especially if your love language is gifts. On the other hand, what happens if your need for love through gifts goes completely unmet?

Like my stepdaughter, my father's parents divorced when he was young. The split was not on good terms, and my grandfather didn't come around much after that. My grandmother was essentially left to raise four kids on her own. Even with the child support she received from my grandfather, it was hard to make ends meet. My grandmother's priority was to keep a roof over her children's heads, clothes on their backs, food in their bellies, and them off the streets of the DC projects. I know she did the absolute best she could do in her situation, and I personally believe she did an amazing job with the hand that was dealt to her during that time. Still, focusing on the necessities had indirect adverse effects on my father, whose love language is gifts. When my dad vocalized his desire for gifts, he was met with chastisement and shame. "Why are you so greedy?" "You always want something for nothing, don't you?" "What have you done to deserve [insert gift here]?" These were the responses my dad received when he asked for love in his love language. The word *gift* comes from a Greek word that means "grace, or undeserved gift"; this makes perfect biblical sense. God's Word tells us that our salvation is a gift from God by grace and cannot be earned by works (Ephesians

2:8–9). If you have to earn a gift, it is no longer a gift but a payment. The response my dad received to his desire for love through gifts was that he did not deserve it—that he hadn't earned it. Add to this the lack of presence of his own father, who moved on with a new wife and stepchildren when my dad was still an adolescent, and the enemy attack is very evident. My father was not only being denied gifts but the other love languages that are needed to make their impact *felt*. The truth of the matter was that my grandmother just didn't have the means to give my father the gifts he desired. It's possible that this caused her some guilt which may have manifested in her harsh responses to my father's requests for gifts—requests for love. Regardless of the reasons, years of this cycle hardened my dad's heart. He became someone who cherished things over people. The childhood attack of his love language caused my dad to value gifts or possessions more than the people in his life. After all, a sixty-inch TV never made him feel unworthy. His three hundred plus pairs of shoes never made him feel like he didn't deserve them. The cycle continued from childhood to adulthood and ultimately into fatherhood. Whenever we asked my dad what gift he wanted for a special occasion, he notoriously replied, "What do you get the man who has everything?" To this day, I cannot determine if that question was rhetorical. My dad's childhood taught him that he wasn't worthy of love, and so he learned to give himself gifts to fill that void. We couldn't give him something that he had already given to himself, which means he wasn't receiving love from us. Even if we tried, he did not appear to truly appreciate the gifts we gave him because he viewed it as our obligation. Worse than that, a threat to his possessions was a personal affront. As children, spilling something on the floor registered as disrespect toward my dad and his house rather than an accident caused by an uncoordinated adolescent. We were attacking his possessions—his gifts to himself—the gifts that never made him feel ashamed or unworthy of wanting them, not like people. The danger of that mindset was that if he perceived anyone as a threat to his possessions, that person became the enemy. These were the love lessons from my dad's childhood—perversion. This revelation about my father is what helped me to begin the journey of forgiving him for his own mishandling of my childhood love language and desiring to repair our father-daughter relationship.

It can be hard for people who love through gifts to acknowledge it because they don't want to appear materialistic. That is yet another way the enemy is able to pervert this love language. If you are a person who loves through gifts, the first step to overcoming the distortion of your love language is to know that there is nothing wrong with it. Desiring gifts from those you love does not make you shallow; it simply means that you desire a reminder of the love you *feel* from that person; love that is wrapped in things like quality time and affirming words, love that served you, and love that touched you deeply. You are worthy of that type of love! The second step to overcoming is to try not to focus on what you did or didn't receive in your childhood. You can't do anything to change that. Instead, focus on the gift of salvation God gave us through His Son—that's the ultimate gift! And if you have not received that gift yet, God is waiting on you to request and receive it. Remember that He created you to love through gifts intentionally. He told us to love our neighbors, and that commandment does not take into consideration their love languages. Loving your neighbor through gifts could give them a memento to remind them of the time you spent with them, the service you provided to them, the kind words you spoke to them, or the warm embrace you gave them. When they look at that gift, they are reminded of the love they *felt* in that moment; the love they *felt* from you. And it's in those moments that they knew you were His disciple (John 13:35), and they *felt* the love of God—that is your purpose!

Chapter 5

Acts of Service: All the Ladies (and Fellas), Who Independent? Throw Yo Hands Up at Me!

Like quality time, acts of service is one of the tougher love languages to speak if you're not fluent in it. *Words of affirmation* can be relatively simple to incorporate consistently. *Quality time* is tougher because of the element of sacrifice it requires from the giver. *Gifts* can be easy to implement once you understand that they must be wrapped in another love language and that it's not the gift itself but what it represents that holds meaning for the receiver. But *acts of service*? This love language must be modeled, acted out, or demonstrated by example. According to Google, an example is "a thing that illustrates a general rule." As Christians, we can consider our "general rule" to be the greatest commandments—love God and love your neighbor—since all our commandments (rules) hinge on these two (Matthew 22:37–40 NIV). For someone who loves in *acts of service*, the "thing" that illustrates this rule is not a word spoken, undivided attention, or an object given, but it is a service that is acted out for the recipient's benefit. The love language of acts of service was beautifully demonstrated by Jesus Himself. The Savior of the world told us that He did not come to be served but to *serve* others and give His life as a ransom for many (Matthew 20:28); because He died, we received the benefit of eternal life through Him. When the disciples questioned

Jesus about who was the greatest among them, He answered that the greatest was the one who *served* in humility (Luke 22:26). He then modeled this teaching through countless examples of His own, including washing the disciples' feet (John 13:3–5, 12–17). Washing a child's feet can seem like a small and even obligatory task to a parent, but it can mean the world to that child if their love language is *acts of service*. *The 5 Love Languages of Children* noted that "in general, parenting is a service-oriented vocation" (p. 91). I know this to be true from firsthand experience as a parent. So, why then do we have so many broken adults that were not adequately loved through *acts of service*? *Acts of service* essentially translates to helping others, and I believe that there are some primary ways the enemy attacks those who need to *feel* love in this way. The first we'll discuss may seem very apparent: if you want to destroy the spirit of an adult who *feels* love through acts of service, do your best to make them *feel* like they're constantly being denied help in their childhood.

Like me, I believe my stepdaughter has more than one primary love language. The enemy did his best to distort her perception of love through gifts as a child, but he didn't stop there. When she was only five years old, he started his attack through acts of service. As a kindergartener, my stepdaughter struggled academically. It was apparent that she did not have a fundamental base in her ABCs and 123s, and it made it hard for her to grasp the material she was being taught. You have to understand that my stepdaughter was, and still is, a very bright young lady. She is highly capable, and her creativity and commitment to the things she's passionate about never ceases to amaze me. I honestly don't know if she ever attended a pre-K program to prepare her for elementary school. What I do know is that at this time in her life, neither of her parents placed a strong emphasis on learning, and neither of them spent a lot of time teaching her these educational fundamentals. I was shocked to learn that my stepdaughter was bringing home failing grades in kindergarten. How was that possible? This was the easy stuff, right? At the time, I was only twenty years old, and her father and I were not yet married. We also lived hours apart in a different city from her for most of her childhood. I did what I was empowered to do from a distance, but to this day I still feel like I could have and should have done more. I wish I had been there more consistently to help her, but I wasn't, and the people that *were* there consistently failed to. If my stepdaughter asked for help with her homework, she would receive responses like, "You're smart enough to figure it out on your own," "I wasn't in class with you so I can't help you," or she would get the help she asked for until she showed her first sign of frustration only to be left to do it herself because of her "bad attitude," and she was just five years old. Worse than any of those responses were that the consequences for continuing to bring home poor grades would often be to take away her possessions or deny her gifts, all the while still not providing her the help she needed. Not only was she being denied help (acts of service), she was also being punished through the withholding of love through gifts. The enemy doesn't fight fair. *The 5 Love Languages of Children* explains that when we serve (help) our children, we teach them how to help themselves and others (p. 94). So the enemy will try to corrupt acts of service in a child's life and replace it with a cycle of rejection. The result of this cycle in my stepdaughter's life was that she learned not to rely on other people for help especially the authority figures in her life. And this did not only apply to her schoolwork. She learned not to ask for help with anything. She would rather struggle than be rejected. She learned to be self-sufficient—no one was going to help her anyway, not even her own parents. Most significantly, she learned to reject wisdom and guidance (help) from those who truly wanted to help her; in her mind they weren't helping her but trying to control her. She became independent to a fault. My stepdaughter eventually overcame her academic obstacles with a lot of hard work, and she started to bring home better grades. In response, she received praise and even gifts. That doesn't change the fact that she didn't receive the help she desired when she needed it the most, and therefore, she didn't *feel* loved. I saw the effects of this perversion of her love language in how she interacted with her little brothers—my sons. She loved them, there's no question about that, but she seemed to resent the idea of being asked to help with them. Why should she have to? She had to figure it out for herself and they needed to learn that lesson too. From a very young age, my stepdaughter was taught that she could not rely on the help of others, so she learned to face everything on her own. But this is not the only way the enemy seeks to pervert love through acts of service.

My mother was still in elementary school when she was identified as a gifted and talented student; her comprehension of the material that was being taught was far beyond her grade level. This designation ultimately led to her having to attend a separate school from the rest of her five brothers and sisters. While they continued at their regular school, my mom attended a school with a more challenging curriculum for kids in her age group (cue sibling rivalry). It's not surprising that my mother's siblings felt jealous over her being singled out as "smarter" than they were, so they treated her like a know-it-all, whether she was truly acting like it or not. What's saddening is that she sometimes received that same treatment from her parents. It wasn't until I was an adult that my mother shared with me one particular experience she had as a child that I believe profoundly altered the way she gives and receives love. She was sitting around the family dinner table with her parents and siblings and needed help with her homework. Since she went to a different school, she was the only one who had that type of homework. My grandmother was helping her as best she could with some math problems, but they weren't getting the right answers. When my mother exclaimed, "But that's not how my teacher said to do it," my grandfather interjected, "If you're so damn smart, why don't you figure it out yourself!" My mom was only in elementary school. It's very likely that my grandfather's harsh response stemmed from his own insecurities of never having finished school. No matter the reason, this exchange both embarrassed and crushed my mom. She told me that from that point on, she never asked my grandparents, especially my grandfather, for help again. In fact, perhaps subconsciously, she became the most helpful of all his children. She was often the only one of my grandfather's children that would help him in the garage while he was working or follow him outside just to see his latest project and how it worked. My grandfather was, and still is, a good man, a good provider, a man of integrity and very humble, but he is not patient and did not "suffer fools gladly" (2 Corinthians 11:19 KJV). Because of this, my mother's siblings chose not to help my grandfather out of fear of receiving a sharp retort or being called stupid for not knowing the difference between a crescent wrench and a pipe wrench—the same type of response my mom got that night at the dining room table. And for all the help my mom gave to my grandfather, he didn't reciprocate it in the ways that she desired. He didn't show up to her basketball games, track meets, or band performances to support her because "if he went to one kid's event, he would have to go to all the kids' events." And while I understand that with six children that would mean a whole lot of events for my grandfather to attend, being at her events would have meant the world to my mom. This is where I believe the cycle of perversion started in my mom's life. Like me, many relationships in my mom's life repeated a pattern that started with her relationship with her father. They were characterized by her going above and beyond to help the other person while they rarely and sometimes never reciprocated it, especially her relationships with men. Because of the response she received from her father as a child, she learned to not to ask for help though she inherently desired it. And it wasn't that she was incapable of helping herself, but to *feel* loved, she needed it modeled by someone acting on her behalf.

I saw this perversion manifest in her relationship with my dad throughout my own childhood. My mom did everything within her power to show my dad love by helping him achieve his wants and desires; this often translated to her spending time and money on material things or a project he wanted completed—remember, my dad's love language is gifts. My dad rarely reciprocated this. If my mom was ever so vulnerable as to ask for my dad's help, he only obliged if he thought the cause was worthy—this made her feel the exact opposite. When she asked him to pick us up after school because we had practice for some activity, he would often decline because he didn't think we deserved to be a part of said activity, and my mom had to rely on other parents to help her out. When she asked him to take us shopping for new clothes, he would refuse because we didn't like the styles he picked for us, so she needed to spend *her* money on the clothes we wanted. My dad even bought groceries just for himself, and it was my mom's duty to grocery shop for the rest of the household. The indirect effect of my mom's distortion of her love language was that she would overextend herself by helping others almost to the point of enabling their lack of reciprocation. Witnessing these frequent inequitable exchanges between my parents served to further pervert my own love language of acts of service. I learned that I could not rely on the help of a man (my partner in a relationship) and that I would have to "handle my business" by myself. This distorted view was reinforced in my relationship with my ex-husband. Though he was much more helpful to me than I had seen my dad be to my mom, it was only in those areas that he felt were worthy. If my ex-husband had to inconvenience himself to help me (or others), he simply would not provide help. I recall a conversation when I was pregnant with our first son where we were discussing the division of our household bills. When we first started living together, our individual incomes were about the same, and so we split the bills fifty-fifty. By the time I was pregnant (almost five years later), my husband was making almost twice my salary. I told him I wanted to discuss redistributing our bills so that I would have more expendable cash after paying my portion. He replied, "That's not my fault, and it's not fair to me. You need to get a better-paying job." His response made me feel worthless, but it was something I had seen play out many times before in my childhood. I wish I could say that this perverted cycle ended with the end of my marriage, but I'd be lying. The same pattern emerged with the men I dated after my ex-husband. They may have affirmed my good qualities and talked to me nicely, but they rarely reciprocated my acts of service. And like my mom, I went above and beyond to prove I was worth their effort, inconvenience, and help while rarely, if ever, receiving it in return. The seed of rejection planted in one generation grew into a full-grown cycle of perversion in the next.

If you have a child that loves through acts of service, understand that the process of loving them by teaching them to help themselves is neither quick nor convenient. It takes time, action, and balance. The enemy will try to slip in any crack you give him to pervert how your child receives this love. So be vigilant, be patient, ready to serve, and willing to help teach them how to help themselves. If you're an adult that has just realized your love language of acts of service was perverted in these very ways, acknowledge it! Acknowledgment does *not* require blame. It is merely a step in the process of asking God to heal you so you can be whole. If you ask for *His* help, He is faithful to never leave you nor forsake you because He is an ever-present help in time of need! Then, be the help to others that you always needed. Help them *feel* the love of Christ. That is your purpose!

Chapter 6

Physical Touch: You
Can't Touch This

According to *The 5 Love Languages of Children*, physical touch is both one of the strongest love languages and the easiest to give unconditionally (p. 30). Unconditional or *agape* love is the type of love God has for us—the type of love we're supposed to give to our neighbors. During Jesus's earthly ministry, He demonstrated this love for us through His healing touch. The Bible recounts many of these healing miracles like Jesus laying hands on the leper (Matthew 8:3), the woman with the issue of blood touching the hem of His garment (Luke 8:43–48), and even Peter extending a healing hand to the lame man at the temple gate (Acts 3:4–7). All these touches led to powerful and restorative healing. Don't miss that! Love through touch can bring physical, emotional, and spiritual healing that makes people whole. The power of *physical touch* is that it can be given in so many ways. It can manifest in hugs and kisses or in a playful wrestling match on the floor. It can be a foot rub after a long day or a simple touch on the shoulder when feeling down. It can be a high-five or holding hands during a stroll in the park. It can also be much more intimate like sex between a husband and wife. All these acts of touch have the power to heal wounds, seen and unseen. But the devil wants us trapped in cycles of hurt. And when there's a literal myriad of ways that love through *physical touch* can be given, it makes sense that there are just as many ways for the enemy to pervert it. Since physical touch is one of the strongest love languages, it's also one that the enemy aims to corrupt the most. His tactics can be overt or subtle, but they almost always originate in childhood.

The adolescent stage is a vitally important time for a girl to receive love and affection from her father; it is crucial for her development of a healthy sexual identity. A lack of affection from her father can have long-lasting effects on a girl's future relationships not only with other men but women as well. Growing up, I always viewed my sister as "daddy's little girl." My dad spent more time with her. He appeared to be more kind to her, and when she was very young, you could often find her curled up in my dad's lap while he was watching a movie. I was jealous. Still, being "daddy's little girl" wasn't enough to save my sister from the corporal punishment that my dad doled out to us almost daily. Those closest to me have heard me say at least once that I got spankings (a whoopin') for everything growing up. This is not an exaggeration, and I wasn't the only one. Bed not made? That's a whoopin'. Chairs not pushed in at the table? That's a whoopin'. Clothes not folded properly in our drawers? That's a whoopin'. Litter box not scooped every hour on the hour (don't forget to initial the chore list to prove you did it)? You guessed it! That's a whoopin'. Forgetting to take out the trash on trash day or not pushing the replacement liner all the way into the trash can? Another whoopin'. Chewing with our mouth open a.k.a. "smacking"? Still a whoopin'. Not announcing ourselves when we entered the house (though we used a key to unlock the door)? That was a thirty-minute lecture about "in-home invasions" and us "disrespecting my dad by playing mind games" and still ended in a whoopin'. My dad was like the Oprah of corporal punishment: "You get a whoopin', you get a whoopin', and *you* get a whoopin'!" Spankings were a frequent occurrence in our household. In fact, it was rarer to end the day without receiving one. I hated growing up like that. Being grounded was a faraway concept and something that "only white parents" did to their kids; I didn't know what "grounded" was, but I knew whoopin's really well. It became a personal challenge of mine to do everything so perfectly that it couldn't possibly result in a spanking. Spoiler alert—still got a whoopin'. Nothing was ever done good enough, and therefore there was always another spanking to be had. For me, it was the constant reinforcement that I was missing the mark that took its toll. My love language was words of affirmation, and though the spankings were painful, the negative words spoken to or about me, my character, and integrity hurt far deeper than my dad's heavy hand on the side of my thigh. But my sister? One of her primary love languages is physical touch. Looking back at our childhood, it makes so much sense. When we still had to share a bed, she never failed to roll right up next to me in the middle of the night, sometimes swinging her leg over the top of my body like I was her pillow. When we no longer shared a bed, she had what seemed like hundreds of stuffed animals on her bed and would always have one of our pet cats sleeping in the bed with her. In fact, when my dad first entered the picture, she was the one that went right up to him and gave him a big ol' hug while I stayed back, shy and hiding behind my mom. My sister needed physical touch to *feel* loved. Instead, what she *felt*, almost every day, was anger and disdain through the touch of our father—perversion. For a child that loves through physical touch, using it to express anger or hostility can hurt them very deeply (p. 40). Physical abuse is detrimental regardless of your love language, but it's especially devastating to those who love through physical touch (p. 30). As mentioned earlier, these interactions can alter how this child relates to people as they grow up. The perversion of my sister's love language definitely had lasting effects into adulthood. Our childhood taught her that a desire for love through physical touch would ultimately be met with hostility and leave her hurting. So, like my ex-husband, she developed a coping mechanism of "going on the offensive". This manifested in my sister rejecting intimacy in the form of physical touch. Instead, since she couldn't control how my dad had treated us, she would control physical touch in an area where so many people operate casually—sex. She became closed off and adept at manipulating people through sex. Her motto was "If we aren't [having sex], why are you touching me?" It was the best way she knew to get the physical touch she really yearned for without having to open herself up to being hurt like she was so many times at the hands of our father. Maybe you wouldn't call what we experienced abuse—I personally never considered it to be—but it was unquestionably excessive. The sad part is that the treatment my dad received in his own childhood and at the hands of *his* father was way worse. My dad was simply repeating the cycle of what he came to know as "normal" or "appropriate" discipline with his children. In his eyes, he was doing better than what his father did to him, and while that may be true, his actions still profoundly affected how my sister gave and received love. Through her relationship with God, my sister no longer views sex as a tool of manipulation. However, she still struggles at times to be vulnerable with her husband due to the fear that those who say they love her (and who she genuinely loves) will most likely hurt her. As for my father, he still battles to this day with the lingering effects of the perversion of physical touch through extreme corporal punishment he experienced in his childhood.

The perversion of physical touch often manifests through some degree of physical or sexual abuse, but it can also result from a lack of physical touch altogether. Maybe you grew up in a household where your parents just didn't show love and affection through touch. Maybe they always supported you and told you how much they loved you. Maybe they bought you gifts and played catch with you. Maybe they never complained about helping you with your science projects. Even your punishments did not consist of spankings or any other form of corporal punishment. Still, what you really needed to *feel* loved was their touch: a hug, a kiss, or snuggle on the couch. If you never got that, it's quite possible that you never *felt* loved. Even this is enough of a foothold for the enemy to corrupt your love language, causing you to try to fill that void in ways that don't line up with God's Word. This could have led to sexual perversion; the enemy appeals to our human nature to convince us that a God promise—unconditional love—can be obtained the devil's way. This perversion could have also presented itself in the form of self-mutilation or harming your own body. The Bible says that our bodies are temples of the Holy Spirit, gifts from God and, as such, our bodies do not belong to us (1 Corinthians 6:19). Our bodies are where the Holy Spirit lives on this earth, and anything we do to desecrate His temple, whether to ourselves or others, grieves Him. If we're not careful to identify destructive behaviors and coping mechanisms for what they are, we will never uncover the true root cause of the problems we face—those problems which seek to destroy our purpose.

If you have just realized that you might be engaging in some of these destructive behaviors due to the corruption of your love language through physical touch, please know that you are not alone. There are many people out there, like my sister, who have endured these attacks from the enemy. The Bible tells us that what the enemy "meant to harm [you], God intended for good to accomplish what is being done now, the saving of many lives" (Genesis 50:20 NIV). What you've gone through—your testimony—uniquely positions you to help bring healing to others. Like Peter with the lame man at the temple gate, you will be able to pass on the love given to you from Jesus by touching other people's lives so that they can be made physically, emotionally, and spiritually whole through Him. *That* has always been your purpose!

Chapter 7

You Are Loved

Have you ever heard of the Word Power Experiment? Well, some years ago, a mother was inspired by a story she read about the residents of an island village and how they "cut" down their trees. So she decided to conduct an experiment with her two children. She placed a red bean on top of a damp paper towel in three separate cups. On one cup she wrote "love," on another she wrote "stupid," and on the other she didn't write anything at all. All three cups were given the same amount of water and sunlight. Once a day her children would take turns speaking to each bean the word written on its cup—no more, no less. Within a few days each bean started to sprout. The bean with no word on its cup and the bean with "stupid" on its cup appeared to be the same size, but the bean with "love" on its cup was a little bit bigger. The very next day, the "love" bean had doubled in size while the "stupid" bean remained the same size it had been the day before. Maybe it was just a coincidence. Maybe the "love" bean was somehow absorbing more sunlight. Maybe. But by the end of the experiment the results were undeniable. The bean with no word on its cup grew as it was expected to, being given daily water and sunlight. The "love" bean grew vibrant and strong. It was twice the size of the bean with no word on its cup. But the "stupid" bean? It never grew any bigger than the size it was when it originally sprouted. In fact, it started to dry and shrivel even though it continued to receive the same amount of water and light as the other two beans.

This experiment was duplicated by many different people and in different environments using a variation of beans, seeds, and plants. No matter the variables, the outcome was always the same. The one that had loving and kind words spoken to it thrived, while the one that received harsh and critical words experienced stunted growth and often wilted.

In the experiments of our childhoods, we are the beans, seeds, and plants in those cups. However, the words that are written on our cups are "words of affirmation," "quality time," "gifts," "acts of service," and "physical touch"—they are our love languages. When we are spoken to in our love language, we thrive and grow vibrant and strong, which enables us to give life to those around us. But when our love language is perverted by the enemy, we can become emotionally, mentally, and spiritually stunted—in danger of wilting and never growing beyond our cups. Every gift, talent, assignment, and connection God gives to us is for the purpose of spreading His Gospel and making disciples through loving one another the way that He loves us. We can speak in tongues, prophecy, possess faith that moves mountains, and even give all our possessions to the poor; but if we don't have love, it means nothing (1 Corinthians 13:1–3). The Bible clearly defines what this love—God's love—is:

> Love is patient, love is kind. It does not envy, it does not boast, it is not proud. It does not dishonor others, it is not self-seeking, it is not easily angered, it keeps no record of wrongs. Love does not delight in evil but rejoices with the truth. It always protects, always trusts, always hopes, always perseveres. (1 Corinthians 13:4–7)

The enemy's goal is to pervert our God-given purpose; to alter, distort, or corrupt what God created us for—to love. Why? Because love covers a multitude of sins (1 Peter 4:8). Because love never fails (1 Corinthians 4:8). Because it's in our love for one another that we prove to the world that we are His disciples (John 13:35 NLT) and *that* love endures forever (1 Chronicles 16:34). *That* is why love is the greatest of all the commandments God has given us. So it is in our childhoods that the enemy attempts to destroy the seedlings of our love for God, our neighbors, and ourselves by altering, distorting, and corrupting the love languages spoken to us and the ones we speak to others, creating cycles of perversion.

As you finish this book, you may have identified some areas in your life where Satan has you trapped, stunted, and wilting. If so, glory to God! You have just made an important step toward uncovering the root of your perversion—acknowledgement. Now the work can begin! Through the Holy Spirit, you can start healing the wounds that were inflicted upon you and those you may have inflicted upon others. You can prevent these wounds from being passed on to future generations. It won't be easy, and it may hurt at times, but growing pains are part of the process. Grow anyway! The pain of growth is far better for you than the pain of continued hurt, dysfunction, and perversion. With the living water of God's Word and the light of the Son, you can be made vibrant, strong, and whole. And it's in your wholeness—in your healing—that you can once again begin to love the way God uniquely created you to. Then you will be fully equipped to establish God's kingdom on earth, and that is the very reason for which you were created. You are loved! Now, go and make disciples...

About the Author

Crystal is the daughter of two retired Air Force veterans and was privileged to live in many places within the United States and England before turning eight years old. Her family was finally stationed in San Antonio, Texas, where she still resides today with her two amazing sons. With her military upbringing and being the eldest of four siblings, she was taught the importance of service early in her life. Crystal is also mixed race and that, along with having lived in many different cities, has given her great perspective on loving her neighbor and having empathy for her fellowmen. She accepted Jesus as Savior at a young age and was raised in the church by her mother. Her passion for community and service led her to cofound a teenage girls' outreach ministry called Caterpillars to Butterflies (C2B) with two of her closest friends and sisters in Christ, and she still actively mentors several young ladies both within and outside of her home church. Crystal has a bachelor of arts in communication studies from the University of Texas at San Antonio, and she recently received her graduate certificate in pastoral counseling from Liberty University. Crystal loves Jesus, her family, and basketball! Go, Dubs! She can often be found having a movie night with her sons or watching any level of competitive basketball. Her writing is also featured in an anthology entitled *She Changed Her Narrative*, which is currently available on Amazon.

CPSIA information can be obtained
at www.ICGtesting.com
Printed in the USA
BVHW032031250521
608118BV00006B/139